Midwhistle

Wisconsin Poetry Series

Sean Bishop and Jesse Lee Kercheval, series editors
Ronald Wallace, founding series editor

Midwhistle

DANTE DI STEFANO

The University of Wisconsin Press

Publication of this book has been made possible, in part, through support from the Brittingham Trust.

The University of Wisconsin Press
728 State Street, Suite 443
Madison, Wisconsin 53706
uwpress.wisc.edu

Gray's Inn House, 127 Clerkenwell Road
London EC1R 5DB, United Kingdom
eurospanbookstore.com

Printed in the United States of America
This book may be available in a digital edition.

Library of Congress Cataloging-in-Publication Data
Names: Di Stefano, Dante, 1978- author.
Title: Midwhistle / Dante Di Stefano.
Other titles: Wisconsin poetry series.
Description: Madison, Wisconsin : The University of Wisconsin Press, [2023]
    | Series: Wisconsin poetry series
Identifiers: LCCN 2022028888 | ISBN 9780299341541 (paperback)
Subjects: LCGFT: Poetry.
Classification: LCC PS3604.I1185 M53 2023 | DDC 811/.6—dc23/
eng/20220914
LC record available at https://lccn.loc.gov/2022028888

for Bill (in his eighth decade on earth)

&

for Dante Jr. (in utero when I wrote this)

Mid-morning, walking ocean shoreline,
I found a hundred blackbirds frozen in ice,
only their heads protruding, black eyes open,
gleaming, most of their sharp beaks still
scissoring in mid-whistle.
—WILLIAM HEYEN, FROM "BLACKBIRD SPRING"

Contents

Midwhistle

i. (out of the azure)

I'm listening to the earth,
    to Bill Heyen read blackbirds
back into the sky above the earth,
        to space junk hurtling over
    the sky, hurtling under it,

while Heyen hurtles through time,
    back to Robert Penn Warren,
back through Auschwitz, through ashes
        to Celan, through Hiroshima
    to Whitman, back through Rumi

to Keats, below the surface
    of Walden Pond, back to woods
stilled in a Long Island night
        seventy years ago. I
    am listening to a man

read himself through remembrance,
    against nostalgia, against
Little Boy, *Enola Gay*,
        & Oppenheimer's sleep.
    I'm listening & trying

to hear myself in old age,
       forty years from now, become
another *This* uplifted, spun
               out of the azure, into
       the syntax of an erased

elegy. I talk there & candle a hope
       for a *One* who no longer
exists. I'm dreaming upstate,
               reading my own blackbirds back
       into my own backbone, back

to those days spent bicycling
       around the neighborhood from
corner store to the oak tree
               by the cemetery gate
       where my brother and I wolfed down

sub sandwiches & let June
       unfold so indolently around us.
Blackbirds flew overhead then,
               in a V, thousands of them,
       as they will tonight when I

put my daughter to sleep, while
       their cawing booms through my skull.
At bedtime, my daughter asks me
               to tell her one more story
       before I can even say "Once

upon a . . ." once, and this is
   the whole interior jewel
& thiefdom of a poem,
         a *Once-before-once* you say
   in the dark because of love.

ii. (an *Unyet* just begun)

I wonder, Bill, how to make
   a poem flare in the dark
out of love & stay lit, though
         the voice cracks and wanes in age,
   that reverse adolescence

that adjuncts the casket's last
   dose of sunlight & weather,
but I must remind myself
         that it is enough to make,
   & dwell in, the music of

a poem for the moment
   of its unfolding without
reaching after some wretched
         shipwrecked urn of an endless
   gathering vast hereafter.

To put it another way:
   there is no *Once* but *This Once*,
no *Ever* but *Now*, no *Then*

or *Than* or *Greater Than Such*
and *Thus* and *Heretofore Hence*

building from lung to larynx.
   I am singing for my wife
& for my little daughter
         & for the fetus growing
   in my wife's belly (for now,

an *Unyet* just begun), for
   my deciduous boyhood
& the boyhoods of my friends
         & brothers, for the girlhoods
   of my wife and mother, for

the infinite riots in
   a sole linden tree's blossom,
for the canticle I held
         in one closed fist as a kid,
   alongside an empty fist,

asking the wind to guess which
   hand it was in, for a boat
a boy once made from a halved
         walnut, bubble gum, & toothpick
   fitted with a tiny kite

of loose-leaf for a topsail.
   I am still sailing that ship,

all my sisters belowdecks,
            the corpse of my father lashed
        to the mast while the sirens,

who are neither meant as myth,
        nor as metaphors, carol
out over the wine-dark seas
            the strange facts of a *What Is*
        that buzzes in the eardrum

of every pregnant moment.
        I wonder if this poem,
and the Each "I" who speaks it
            through, & through it, has gone too
        irrevocably astray,

but the preoccupation
        of this poem, its initial
impetus & its lone aim
            was to talk across time, Bill,
        to the you at twenty-four,

beginning a journal aimed
        at your grandchildren & I
(& the multitudes any
            one reader incarnates as
        audience). I see you, through

the haze of cigarette smoke
    & poker games, already
in your midtwenties, holding
        the long woolen lapel of
    a kind of ambition that seams

itself as an alphabet
    of sorrow and enduring.
I see you—perched urbanely—
        between Anne Sexton & Al
    Poulin at the Brockport

Writers Forum, the three of
    you discussing confession
a handful of years after
        M. L. Rosenthal criticked
    confessionalism to life.

The thin black necktie of your
    apprenticeship had not been
taken off yet, & yet you
        hold forth with a quiet poise,
    which would have been beyond me

at that age, maybe at this one.
    There is so much life to live
& die into in an hour.
        Kafka's phrase comes to mind: "In
    the struggle between yourself

& the world, hold the world's coat."
　　Perhaps, that's the real aim of
this poem: to hold the world's coat.
　　　　No, that's not right; the phrase is
　　incidental. The real aim

is to talk to you, myself,
　　is to talk myself to you
without being too inward-
　　　　turned, & returning without.
　　Again, I think of you, Heyen,

sitting in your easy chair,
　　in the single-line couplets
of a cadence all your own,
　　　　ensconced in the mastery
　　of eighty years harkening

to the blue hour hidden in
　　the yolk of a syllable,
counting syllables inside
　　　　the hour of that syllable,
　　unpeeling an undersong

just below the audible,
　　just beyond the eye & ink
& the symmetry & lack
　　　　of line bivouacked upon line.
　　I am there whittling your face

into my grandfather's cane,
  thirty years ago, as he
told a story from his war,
    something about the tattoos
  on prisoners' arms after

they were liberated from
  the camps. I can't quite recall
his words, the story, cinder
    now, a mouthful smoldering
  in the obscurity of

a century that's not done
  with us just yet. Kafka died
almost a decade before
    the Nazis came to power.
  His fragments were like that poem

by Adam Zagajewski
  trying to praise the suture
& the wound, the thrush lost in
    the mulberry bush, the world
  mutilated as it is,

the unfinished & broken
  as ethic & aesthetic,
the only healthy response
    to a diseased & dying
  planet in its pinprick of

a galaxy tucked inside
　　God's own sewn-shut breast pocket.
I am breaking always, as
　　　　you are too, into other
　　selves & asymmetries & such.

This universe, as such, is
　　only one among many,
this multiverse is all one,
　　　　& I & you & we, they
　　retrace our snowshoed steps back

to the infinite *Now* of
　　a phoneme stuck in the throat.
Bill, your blackbirds frozen in
　　　　ocean waves keep returning
　　to me, their immobile beaks

petrified into endless,
　　soundless, screeching I can't mute,
or unmute, for that matter.
　　　　My wife & I will be joined
　　by a newborn soon, due on

August 9th, the day we wed,
　　anniversary also
of Nagasaki's bombing,
　　　　a reminder of how all
　　dates, calendars, & nations

mine & scar & tentacle,
     how the memorial impulse
mocks, even as it unearths,
          how a vow contains its own
     arsenic "I do" in it,

&, yet, how shabby our lives
     would be if we didn't dare
avow ourselves, to husband
          & wife ourselves with a faith
     in the wound happiness makes.

iii. (interlude: elegy for Adam Zagajewski)

The homesteads stay abandoned.
     The stylish yachts sail onward.
The refugees continue
          their toilsome journeys nowhere
     & the borders have been closed

& arrayed with bright cages.
     The executioners still
sing as they sharpen their blades.
          A Chopin nocturne spins out
     into the stratosphere. Time

skills itself with the griefs of
     one thousand thousand mothers.
The pocket watches all run

backward toward the volta,
backward toward the volta,

of a distant century.
    The sunflowers bow their heads
like medieval friars begging
        the scorched earth for sustenance,
    astonishment, & release.

I am, as you are, a child
    of cello, air, & mint spears
that light my tongue with Augusts
        I would like always to keep
    in the pulse of this poem.

I am writing for the ghost
    of a lucid moment, a thought
bound to the most radiant
        crescent moon that watched over
    the country of my exile

in the seconds before I
    was born. I am writing to
praise the faces of mothers,
        the scent of wild lavender,
    the dove in the violin

whose coo recalls my heartbeat.
    Remember, a nocturne twirls

in the heart of the homesteads
　　　　where the refugees unsing
　　the border, the cage, the blade.

iv. (this mattering of music)

Our *Unyet*, Bill, is a boy.
　　In the ultrasound pictures
he looks like an aerial
　　　　view of a giant island
　　in a little lake just now,

& if current events tell
　　us anything, it's that points
of view matter urgently,
　　　　and that we are not islands
　　the sea slowly swallows up,

but either a Pangea,
　　or an archipelago,
of competing needs & nos
　　　　& grievances & yeses,
　　& this was the case before

the pandemic & always.
　　It's true: our nation always
spoke the language of zip tie
　　　　& riot, of shackle, pledge,
　　& endless blocked amendment,

& it is easier to
    uncotton to such unjust truths
that make America's great
        idiom a shared awkward
    admission of guilt & grief

lighting the tongue from sea to
    shining & other traumas,
but I look to him (my unborn).
        I hear in the unrung bell
    behind the lines of this poem,

a voice, a shapeless flame, one
    note repeated in all poems,
love, this flowering promise,
        this mattering of music,
    the unnamed fact of him, fire—

Bill, I think of your meetings
    with James Dickey, his falling
stewardesses & blind kids
        beating their closed eyes beneath
    my own sleep-shuttered eyelids.

Can a poem one day blitz
    & undo the language of
warfare shotgunned into half-
        time & pastime & pregame,
    the way a tailgate might un-

hinge itself on the starlight
    of a syllable you hut,
hut, hike from the diaphragm,
          & drift back in the pocket,
    & dispocket in the drift,

scanning the routes all poems
    take from air to hand to end-
zone? We poetry lovers
          are all wide receivers, out
    in the open, hands outstretched,

rewriting the audible
    in our bellies, undoing
the rote logic of playbooks,
          improvising the motion
    whistling through our own muscles.

Sing for us, the dragonfly
    in the arc of an anthem,
the bumblebee zigzagging
          the sidelines of an empire.
    I praise your *Lord Dragonfly*,

Bill, & praise the ambition
    it must take to un-Amherst
a clover & a bee from
          the funerals in a brain,
    from the prairie and its yawp.

Are we all just corporations
    of want & want & desire
& compete & cut & die
        & rot & rise tomorrow
    anew, defiant, refreshed?

Again, Bill, I'm thinking of
    you & the perfect spiral
Dickey hurled in your poem
        to Merwin, itself spiraled
    out, unraveling right here.

How he could suspend a sled
    burial in melody
with a dream ceremony
        & how you leapt from his voice
    to your father's dying bed

& your brother Werner's ghost,
    which reminds me of the phrase
tossed off in a friend's poem:
        we "talk to other the ghosts,"
    we poets, when our wives are

asleep, when our husbands snore,
    when our restless children toss
their dreams in a tight spiral,
        spiraling back into lines
    raveled in our fingertips.

We poets talk to ourselves,
    talking to the past, to those
heroes and mentors who light
            our way, who we walk off from—
    we talk to other the ghosts.

v. (soundtrack for a zombie apocalypse)

I start, Bill, by gathering
    paradise, my son, & you,
my friend, into a note, a chord,
            an onslaught, a choir of trees
    & tree houses & wind through

treetops. A single image
    inspires an Edda of sound.
Query a superior
            cataclysm. Make your own bed
    of longing & want & need

& kneed & needle a groove
    onto calloused fingertips.
All flight takes off from there, this:
            the innate loneliness of
    a plucked string, its throb & quiver

& quake & steadily thrummed
    being. Music rearranges
the atoms in the convex

mirror I hold up to view
the expanding universe

in my basal ganglia.
Ferry yourself in reverse,
back from the land of the dead.
Every day begins in death
& ends in resurrection.

I am zip-lining toward
salvation, apocalypse,
an indolent Saturday
afternoon in October.
There's so much melody in

the world & so little time,
so many clichés, so few
Earth-altering asteroid
impacts. I gather the stars
in this strumming, let them shine.

The poplars in me blaze up,
another season's ending,
interminable August
I keep athwart & dying
into, a fawn that still lifts

her head as if in deep prayer,
as if further to nuzzle

me into a truth about
        place & forgetting & myth.
    I've fashioned myself laurels

of magnolia, matins
    of starling & scuppernong.
A *Might Could* juked from the beak
        of an egret will become
    my querulous epitaph.

I love hill country & swamp
    alike. Blood sage & wild thyme
syncopate the yearning in
        my heartbeats & aches & aches.
    I want to formulate home

as one long winding sentence
    written in black oil paint on
the white walls of a study,
        a carbine in the corner,
    bullets lined up like little

rogue dioramas, this life
    a fable in the lungs of
an angry prophet, the son
        of a preacher, a gator
    writhing on the riverbank,

&, meanwhile, the whole hot blind

Earth turned rowdy cotillion,
father cardinal turning
            into a bellflower's bloom,
    a stag's breath pluming the dawn.

Some days, dread hallelujahs
    & whatnot build in my throat
& I find myself humming
            against a nostalgia
    I would permanently ban

in favor of the warm glow
    inside a note, like the first
time I met my wife, or when
            my two-year-old used to fall
    asleep with my finger clamped

in her little hand. & if,
    Bill, you look up quickly,
in those moments (like this one),
            you can hear the moon render
    itself—in vibrato, shrills,

bridges, unaccountable scales,
    a whole powerful winding
octave of arcane, antique,
            recondite, soaring, feral,
    peregrine sounds—an epic.

&, Bill, I feel a hatchet
   cleaving my gray matter while
the white house inside my skull
         burns down & I'm stuck between
   brick & chain link wondering,

not wondering, just blanking
   into white noise & white space
& pundits become kudzu
         around the magnolia
   tree of my torso. I feel

a murder of white horses
   ridden by drunk laureates
galloping the fugitive
         dark & contending to sing
   from there, under the mushroom

cloud of an alternative
   history, while the footage
from Charlottesville rolls after
         the fiction, before the flag.
   Here's song notes for the soundtrack

to the end of an empire:
   "The ghost of a church bell should
ring out in the refrain &
         an unspent shotgun shell should
   be placed on the windowsill

above the kitchen sink, next
    to a Matchbox car & an
origami swan on fire.
        If a melody threatens
    to ballad & unmap itself,

gerrymander yourself in
    a puff of dandelion
seeds & ride the wind as breath
        or prayer, or just plain exhale"
    these stepped septasyllables.

vi. (interlude: to my wife)

In this universe, black holes
    spaghettify hapless stars.
Butterflies drink turtle tears.
        If you took all the empty
    space in our atoms out, all

the human beings on earth
    could fit in a sugar cube.
These days, I feel like I have
        all the time in the world, &
    none. Last night our sweet daughter

came to sleep in our bed, &
    she was afraid & sniffly,
the ark of her three-year-old

body a slight boat between us.
   & as the seconds slowed down,

I felt gravity's dull pull
   ensnare & stretch me into
a long noodle of sunlight.
         I knew that this moment was
      paradise & that dying

might only be a kind of
   devouring of the distance
between atoms in teardrops.
         I want to kiss your open
      mouth as your snores mingle with

my snores & the dreaming dog's
   whimpers & our daughter's sighs
& our son's fetal heartbeat
         keeping time steadily inside
      your adorable belly.

I am a sum of what loves
   have been drummed forth & nurtured
into shining by the worlds
         you have spun out & held in
      a rapturous unseen hour.

A bouquet is not enough thanks.
      Instead, take the vase of these

folded hands, a hummingbird
        levitating between palms,
    its hundred hundred wingbeats

as rubied as pomegranate
    seeds, as electric as song
rising from a sugared tongue.
        I'm drunk on our universe,
    our hapless stars & turtle

tears & butterflies & black
    holes & sugar cubes & you,
our *Unyet* son, lemon-sized,
        amniotic cosmonaut,
    cresting event horizon.

vii. (from aster)

This is the first long poem
    addressed to an old poet
(forgive me) & a fetus
        at the same time. I wander
    the miles from umbilical

to octogenarian
    & I come back, Bill, to stairs,
abysses, apples, blackbirds, bows
        & ribbons during the Gulf
    War. Bergen-Belsen whines like

a missile, you said, & that
    caretaker you met haunts me,
how he might transplant a shrub
        & find a fragment of bone,
    a shell casing, a tin cup,

a wedding band, the debris
    of *Shall Remember* written
in red on a shaft of white
        marble, sprung from the sentence
    those words moor to history.

& now, Bill, speaking of this,
    I want to speak directly
to my unborn son, to hold
        out for him some directives
    for raking through the heather—

Learn, from aster, bluebonnet,
    & wisteria, how to
ungrope, from earth to air, this
        motion called blooming. Learn to
    small talk like sunflower to

acre upon acre in meadow
    after meadow of your heartbeat.
Son, you carry a bespoke
        heartland beneath your rib cage,
    homespun, ecstatic galaxy

of milkweed & goldenrod
   & garden phlox, a redwing
in a Heyen strophe soaring
        heavenward. Son, flirt only
   in the style of trillium

with breeze near wild blackberries
   that will sugar the tongue with
possibility's fairer
        house. Remember, there are ferns
   in you, & lilies bending

in the underbrush, & sun-
   light, genuflecting to thorn
& morning glory alike.
        Remember the whimper of
   the wolf cub, the power of

a grizzly's paw, the soft muzzle
   of a coyote curled within
your chest. Harass only that
        which degrades you, turning you
   against lightning & thunder,

blizzards flurrying the tundra
   in your head. The mesas sing
in baritone: "Whoever
        degrades another degrades
   me." & the stars & crickets

tempest another blue hour.
   Son, learn to be completely
alone in the storm. Learn to
         be faithful to the gentle
   animal within. Know you are

loved & so, must love the way
   the wilderness loves, as sprig
after sprig shooting through soil,
         a perfect prayer for moonlight
   & daydream hidden in root

& stamen, budding sudden
   lazuline & horizon pink
at nightfall & further day-
         break. You will find, little one,
   it's hard to keep the human

close to the ground & nested
   in orchard & fen & in
the neighborhoods you grow up
         adventuring through, Bill's woods
   or mine, or Thoreau's, or Frost's.

viii. (poetry, be my body of shining)

I read slave catchers were called
   blackbirds and, of course, there was
the other pandemic: there

were the days I couldn't write
about & images that breeched

the interior kingdom
of a leaving. I wanted
to change, Bill, the whole arc of
American history.
I wanted to reread *Leaves of*

Grass as if it were sung by
Billie Holiday backward
& underwater, under
the brined hull of the schooner
Phillis while the great whites swooped

& circled the waters chummed with
the original disease
of—your line comes to mind: "Walt's
brine grew seaweed in us"—yet
I wanted not to cancel

anything. I wanted to
reverse the recoil of this
constant tragic reveille
we wake into pledge & oath.
I wanted change to, to, to

hold the world in a tiny
infinitude of tracks, to

dwell in the singing of it
    forever. There was pain, fear,
  & hopefulness & I spent

my time reading & walking
  & arguing with myself
& loving my family
    as you have done, Bill, for eight
  decades. I spent my time hurt

& dying & thrumming with
  song. I wanted to hold it
all, everything in its
    fullness, to keep all of this
  music from slipping through my

ephemeral arteries.
    Still, the heartbeats of my wife
& my little girl, my unheard
    son ghosting the amnion,
  the panting dog at my leg

under the kitchen table
  & the stuffed animals so
abandoned at naptime on
    the hardwood floors & (two blocks
  over) the lawn mower's hymn

& the chorus of chain saws,

slicing through the rotting two-
by-fours of the neighbor's deck,
            possessed an almost past tense
      untenable sweetness. Why

am I always descending
      the same staircase & coming
into these vocal structures
            over & over from new
      angles & angels & angels?

I am telling you I love
      & love & love, despite my
dying, despite my breaking,
            despite the blinking cursor
      at the end of the text &

the horror of white noise &
      the engulfing Molotov
sadness of this second. It's
            heartening when monuments
      topple, when the streets intone

uprising, when masked & angry
      the avenues teem with
outrage. I am listening
            on repeat, to these same sweet
      sad melodies, to these

same golden-voiced horns, to these
    arpeggios of need
& want & throb & squawk &
        must & salient return.
    Fear girds me & I recall

myself again—that I have
    always been here on the verge
of understanding, but not
        dipping in, instead, staying
    in wonder & the spell of

this aria in my chest,
    these blackbirds & the feeling
that although these words are not
        enough, I will utter them
    & dwell in the culvert of

their utterance. I will one
    day die & enter into
another trilling field of
        undoing. The urge to keep
    all the atoms of the *What*

I think I am is strong. I
    wish we were all better than
I am or you or we, in
        our pursuits & quarrels &
    cyclically unfolding

quivers of wounds & wounds &
    wounds, but I am, as we are,
the kind of ones who suffer
            our way into the sunlight,
    perhaps, & in the next blank

broadside, I hope I am changed.
    Let me be more loving, more
open and less openly
            trying to please or like.
    Let me thank. & I pray &

I pray & I pray: the *I*
    can't breathe of a national
pastime, which is nothing but
            an abattoir—& George Floyd
    hearkening back to those in

the cargo hold of slave ships,
    the aforementioned schooner
Phillis, the poet singing
            in the darkness the anthem
    of an unknown, unsaid, as

yet unfounded country with
    chokeholds & thresholds, threshing
rooms & killing floors, all
            these griefs clustering, & the
    *we the*s & the *me*s & the

*you*s putting in our two cents
    & then recalling greater
griefs in the heart of the heart-
        land I carry (as you do)
    beneath my Kevlar, so snug,

so securely suburban
    & so cosmopolitan
& verved into a nightmare
        logic of forgetting—yet
    for all the amnesia:

poetry, be my body
    of shining. Those moments of
brotherhood, thrived youthfulness,
        & the yawning puppy-eyed
    feeling of rooftops & yawps

& mandolins in daydreams
    & the feeling of beauty
in the bones of a poem.
        We are, I am, born for more
    than suffering and glory,

yes, just wonder rioting
    staccato with enormous
savoir faire the middle part
        of a *yes yes yes*, sends me
    back to the final words of

"On a Painting by DeLoss
    McGraw." In blue ink, Heyen,
your baseball card poem ends:
        "Beyond us all, history
    seethes + blossoms." & I pray.

ix. (a forty-three-second free fall)
"Excessive self-consciousness
    is debilitating for
the poet," you said, Bill, in light
        of atrocity's lyric
    potential & the practice

of poetics engaging
    with the murderous present
bygone impending Today.
        We are always stuck in ice,
    caught between the reticent

earth & the ocean of mind
    & heart, rendered as impulse
to affirm, proclaim, to praise
        & to rage against the pull
    of an arctic undertow,

which is what? The bullshit of
    this saying & not saying?
This poem flailing back to

blackbird & the dove inside
a turtledove, a dovecote,

a dovetail where the unnamed
congregate & protest fire
in the flame's *redwhite&blue*
center. I contain redtail
& redcoat alike. I am

my own Founding Father. So
are you. I am Bill Heyen,
invited over to eat
at Allen Ginsberg's table,
straightlaced in my tweed blazer

& brush cut & Germanic
American smile. I am
Crispus Attucks gunned down by
the British in the Boston
Massacre. I am Chester

A. Arthur on Air Force One,
eating KFC, bucket
after bucket of drumsticks,
factory farmed, delicious,
which is to say my country

implicates me in its graft
& guilt & lust, & turns me

into a victim, a crime,
an absolute allegiance
to slur & imprecation,

a state one poem or an-
other might let me outwit.
When I close my eyes, I see
a mushroom cloud billowing
up from Nagasaki, from

the ladybug that landed
on my wife's dress on the steps
of the courthouse (or was it
a church?) on our wedding day,
from my wife's uterus, from

the uncut umbilical cord,
from the dilated cervix,
from the unborn's newborn cry,
& back to blackbird shadows
burned into the temple walls,

into brutalist facades
of state university
libraries, into the arcs
& arks & architecture
of a narrative uncoiled

away from the *Us* who sits

in an easy chair & scribes
the day, in all its minute
       detail, as daily routine.
    Each letter of this poem,

itself a blackbird flying
    into itself, into its
own motionless-winged shadow.
       & again, Bill, I'm reading
    shadows in an interview

where you say, "I still believe
    that only poetry can
save the human world. But I'm
       not talking about our word
    constructs, lyric & other

poems that we read & write,
    but about a poetic
conception of our place
       here, of the earth as One, of
    thought as an integration

until we realize we must change
    or we will die out." I too
believe in poetry as
       a metapoetics of
    change, space where blackbirds dissolve

in a flash, atomize, & dance
    themselves into flight patterns,
as yet unthought and unsung,
        where Fat Man falls upward,
    a forty-three-second free-

fall into *Bockscar*'s bomb bay,
    as the shadows of blackbirds
unburn themselves from the once-
        walls of a cathedral turned
    to detonated rubble.

x. (mellifluous blah-blah // time travel)

The rubble reassembles
    itself. I fly back into
myself like an old blackbird
        hyphening the power lines
    with its hollow bones & quills

uninked but blooded in flesh.
    I have perhaps lost my way
in this long poem & won't
        find an exit, a dismount
    fitting the poet being

addressed—William Heyen? Or
    the William Heyen inside
a Heyen poem? Or myself?

The "I" who is, and is not,
I? Am I a blackbird's song?

Or another someone else
    entirely decomposing
in this very poem's core?
        I am unsure of it all,
    as usual, but the poem

reassures without surety
    or fealty or the promise
of remuneration. Still,
        I hope none of this comes off
    as a "mellifluous

blah-blah," to quote you again.
    Merwin wrote to you to say
he wanted only to write
        what might be carried in times
    of threat and crisis, what might

wing out into great peril.
    Are there territories now,
austere enough to fill with
        the belligerence and song
    of the springs you've recorded?

In your long poem to him,
    you catalog a life lived

in literature, nights with
         James Wright, letters from MacLeish,
    martinis with Anne Sexton,

and so much more aglow in
    the Rembrandt amber of
the century of the dream songs
         & death. I am praying in
    the pit where Radnòti's last

poems absorbed the music
    of the anonymous dead
& scissored that music
         into a frozen timeless
    horror of eternity.

Under my closed eyelids now,
    your blackbirds fly, freeze again,
screech into my temporal
         lobe the aria of rage
    & need & want that rewrites

this poem as it's composed,
    as it flies south & north, west
& west & west in its own
         sprung manifest destiny,
    its frontier thesis logic

of defining a body

against the wilderness sprawled
beyond its artificial
        edge. Let there be no border
    between poem & self, but

no celebration either
    of such comingling. Let us
time travel together, Bill,
        to that dimension before
    birth, where my unborn child drifts

now through the ether, & where
    I was once, & you were once,
the ellipsis of a *Not-*
        I repeated, the way the
    "the" gets repeated in that

poem of yours in response
    to Stevens, that clever the
the stuttering its flowered
        fulfillment over the ends
    & beginnings of your lines.

xi. (interlude: on rereading Anne Carson's Sappho)

At twenty, the [brackets] meant
    so much less, having never
held a deep loss in a closed
        palm, having never beckoned

gaps into garlands, having

never sprung what was missing
   into a holy phoneme
caught in the throat, unsounded,
      stillborn, calling out through scrolls
   of a blinking cursor. Now,

almost two decades later,
   the white space fills with the white
noise of a life, the ache of
      fragment stacked upon fragment,
   the choke of arrivals lit

from the start with the heat of
   leaving, too many stairwells
walked down, too many frail
      hellos, hospice beds whose sheets
   went unwrinkled because death

came too soon. Want calls out now,
   summoning the soft hip curve
of lover after lover,
      friend after friend, like a chain
   of paper dolls stretched from

margin to margin & set
   ablaze. The lacunae bloom,
violets in the lap of

a ruinous god. Say this:
What is no longer is dew

& nectar & gold & plucked
rose petals gone somnolent
in the wind. Say: Winter. Say: If
        not, shine. Say: Alive is more
    than enough. Say: Regret tastes

of anise and pebble. Say:
    ]
]
        ]
    love, nimble, astray, poor, pour:

xii. (in a millisecond's ark // when asked to describe the self // *Yojimbo* // Ishmael)

Love, nimble, astray, poor, pour:
    I spend hours, Bill, as you did
once, some five decades ago,
            translating the patois of
    my three-year-old daughter's talk.

I can't understand every
    word, but the feeling always
tends toward velocity.
            Pink motorcycles climb castle
    walls & vanish, an acorn

transforms into a spaceship,
  battalions of chipmunks
suddenly appear, the paint
      swirls off a canvas, kisses
    the air that makes an open

doorway, & turns it purple.
  She opens doors & closes
them. She turns rocks & fathers
      & trees & mothers into
    eggshell & duckbill yellow.

Key moments coast the rising
  action & sometimes it seems
all denouement unraveled
      in gibberish arias.
    Listening, a world opens

to the universe ending
  inside an atom, the big
bang of the earth forever
      imploding & reassembled
    in a millisecond's ark.

Inevitably, I stare
  at the horizon and say:
"mulberry fields." They're always
      so dramatic, these acts
    of self-definition. Time,

that portly innkeeper, pours
 another cup of rice wine
& you know that somewhere deep
   inside your katana-drawn
 mind a duel begins & ends

in an instant. In fact, we've
 faked our deaths one thousand times
before the showdown. A wind
   whistles its theme song off-screen
 & I think of my father

watching *High Noon* at midnight,
 years before he died, & me,
sitting beside him in one
   of those rare wordless eras
 of armistice between us.

I am left with a few frames,
 a fool beating a prayer drum,
a wild dog clamping a chopped-
   off hand in his mouth, a close-up
 on an assassin's handsome face.

My father's assassin face,
 which looked exactly like mine,
presages my son's. He will
   share my name, this junior who
 will turn me senior, chrism

me an internal change like
     grace wrung from the sacraments
in my father's faith. Will this
          son of mine look like me, like
     my father did, or I him?

Is resemblance contagion?
     Inheritance? Atavism?
Legacy? I trace the lines
          of my face in the mirror,
     a door where father turns son.

& did you, Bill, resemble
     a father or a son?
& what were your teenage years,
          from the McCarthy hearings
     to the Little Rock Nine? What

did you make of all that was
     making you? All the pivots
& riots, & the bullets,
          the handsome-faced assassins?
     & did you dream of Melville

as I did in upstate New
     York? A dream half-hidden in
the world he predicted, the one
          we live in now?
     I remember those stairwells:

my bedroom's slanted ceiling
    turned lyric-thrashed rib cage
of a leviathan. Raged
        with want, my teenage body,
    a perfect sermon for sharks,

hived my mind with subtlety
    (or was that some other tome?).
My heart turned daft mutineer,
        turned mangy old castaway,
    turned overboard renegade,

treading water in the wake
    of some girl I can't recall
anymore, but who loomed like
        a harpooneer in my dreams.
    All of adolescence is

just such an anatomy,
    a text whose ornate surface
you spear & misconstrue in
        vibrant disconcert with spells
    of detail that overwhelm

& render unconscious, just
    as the arc of a pattern
begins to unwhite itself
        on the insides of your eyelids.
    How many permutations

of a self did I sift through
to get from there to this place
where I am my own coffin-
buoyed salvation & shipwrecked
fore & aft, my own crow's-nest

view of a life's undoings
& missteps? How the flower
& gentle heat of my wife's
soft exhalations beside
me at night somehow rewrites

all the anguish of homeroom
& twin bed & reverie,
I'll never quite know. How strange
to find yourself bedfellow
to a past's italic type

set against an unquoted
imperative first sentence:
call me, call me, call me, call—
the sound of that last line,
a merl of blackbirds, flying.

xiii. (skilled with moons)

A merle of blackbirds, flying,
conjures up, apropos of
nothing, the *Don Quixote*

I read myself into at
around the same time Melville

dreamed me into forecastle
    & topsail. Those pages shine.
Long before the long defeat
        of the body that begins
  in middle age, the awkward

want of adolescence queues
    the synapses of the brain
to the electric excise
        of fang & horn & tusk trussed
  to such unknowing. Back then,

in bed, a sarcophagus
    in afghan, the yellowing
paperback below the dull
        halo of a flashlight, to
  become was easy & cut

deep. It was a knighthood, this
    knowledge of a story's heart-
beat & ache, a chain mail of
        mirrors, the lost baby teeth
  of old age, the decayed spot

under an apple's luster,
    the skin of a myth I could

crawl inside, skilled with the moons
		of my own imagining,
	in a crescent of blackbirds.

xiv. (playlist on repeat)

I dissolve your blackbirds back
		into a crescent, into
	one note "singing in the dead
			of night." The bright red gashes
		of a pop song subsuming

themselves in superior
		rhythms, the rhythms of your
	single-line couplets, the happy
			geniuses of your woodlot
		calling back to the "Danse Russe"

of that other William, who
		won the Pulitzer the year
	before you started keeping
			your journal, but whose body
		of work supersedes any

prize & whose naked dancing
		before the mirror of these
	words strangely reassures me,
			validates the vocation
		we share, & you share with those

other Williams you one-upped
        John Logan's other-Johns with,
your Blake to his Keats, Shakespeare
                to Milton, Donne to Wordsworth—
        add Merwin & Heyen, too.

But away from naming, from
        the enduring Florentine
and his terza rima to
                the cantos in my unborn's
        rapidly expanding lungs.

There's so much we have written
        into ourselves—we crouch, no,
float, like little untethered
                astronauts at open front
        school desks hidden deep within

& scratch out these desperate
        missives—dispatching ourselves
further & further into
                our snagged selves. I am need.
        I am a poem of need.

What I need is a volta
        every other syllable
like Hopkins. I am full of
                lilac, arnica, eyebright
        like Celan's medicine in

the poem. I gather thus
   a bouquet made of broken
rusty bits of barbed wire dug
        out of the earth. I look up
   & see the spot where the star

of Bethlehem once, & will
   again, most likely, with
grace & audacity, shine.
        Over that spot I see feathers,
   drifting down like big snowflakes

forming in a pointillist
   self-portrait of my son's face
forty years from right now,
        when I'm your age, Bill, & he
   is mine, & our fathers have

alchemized in watershed
   & rubied themselves into
a line from Kabir, warbling
        an anonymous opus
   back into the vertebrae.

xv. (little arks)

Back into the vertebrae,
   poetry taught me a line
might buck against the vast blank

expanse of a page. The vast
blank expanse of the page makes

a mountain bed. An adolescent "I" sleeps
there, inside the infinite
umbers of Caravaggio,
my own mythology scraped
with a painter's putty knife.

I'm typing this into a Word
document & can't picture
a world without a blinking
cursor at the beginning
& end of composition.

In 1964, smudged
ink was cursor & the phrase
"Word document" redundant.
We've lost & gained so much, Bill,
traveling as we have now

from *Then* to a future, where
the soft glow of screens becomes
context & window onto
the wild unhinged unwinding
flap of imagination.

Those nights, I sat on the porch
of the self, & looked at how

icicles hung from the eaves,
        return me to the wild unhinged.
   When I first started writing

poetry, nothing I wrote
   made sense, then it made too much
sense. Now, I have settled in.
      I am taking the feeling
   out & letting small slivers

of light striate my heart,
   which is only a muscle
the size of a fist pumping
      a red essential music.
   As you wheel, poem, poet

insane for light, so do I,
   antic scraps of silk, jeté
of those little girls daughters
      will always be & blossom
   from, little arks hulled with moon.

xvi. (after Anthony Brunelli's *Depot at Dusk*)

As an awkward teenager,
   I walked that bridge a thousand
times, turning like those cop cars
      rampant with speed, reaching west
   like those train tracks arrowed on

hems of horizon. Back then,
   I was full of unwieldy
reverences for ruin,
        for scenes of dereliction
   freighted with ordinary

awe, psalms of corrugated
   steel, gospels of cracked asphalt
& abandoned factories.
        My father, grandfather,
   & great grandfather worked

a block from the vista in
   Brunelli's painting, as cooks,
clerks, railway men—the diner
        lost behind the painting's gaze.
   It's gone now, as are those men

& their wives (except for my mom),
   their world as distant as
the smell of fresh sciachiatta
        baking in my grandmother's
   kitchen on 20 Linden Street,

those three decades ago. There's
   no painting to hold that world
in place, no way to bring back
        those faces, the chipped bone china
   of their voices, forever

packed away, stowed in the attic
    of my brain. Bill, Realism,
Wallace Stevens said, corrupts
        reality, & by this
    I think he meant a dove in

the belly can tell you more
    about life than the pigments
in an accurate art. In
        the painting, my hometown is
    as it was & is & is

not & never was, this stark
    vivid mundane blue hour I
would sink into, this sermon
        of graffitied midday sun,
    the legacy of swamp-root

mountebanks & immigrant
    angels, a destiny of
manifested desire I
        carried unwittingly at
    eighteen, at seventeen, at

sixteen, at every age
    I walked where the engines of
the Norfolk Southern shaclacked
        through my veins. I walked wifeward
    & daughterward & sonward,

dogward, poetward. I walked
    with my loved ones' likenesses etched
on every atom of me,
            ached, just so, alive, drawing me,
    gently, home. & here at home

I sit in my basement, this
    long poem unfolding on
a screen next to Bill Heyen's
            mammoth books & some letters
    he sent me (you sent me): one

that told me to go back into
    this aria (which began
as a ten-page sortie, rife
            with blackbirds & becoming)
    & suggested the cinquain.

You ended that letter with:
    "How the fuck did I get to
be 80?" & also, words
            of love for MacLeish, Wilbur,
    Merwin, Stafford, & others

who lit your way, as you are
    lighting mine. We are going
up the stairs & down in this
            poem, repeating ourselves
    to get someplace, elsewhere, new,

eighty, forty-two, twenty-eight
    weeks. We talk through ourselves to
other the ghosts, blackbirds,
        apples, stairwells, cattle cars,
    maggots, bulldozed mud within.

Maggots, bulldozed mud within,
    a couplet from '67
in your journal comes to me:
        "I know no other, better
    ways, / to toll what the awkward

heart says." I'm there with you, Bill.
    I'm here, tolling my heart out,
five lines at a time, these rooms
        filled with the furniture of
    my needs & other blackbirds.

I need bikes & flowering
    grasses to be eternal,
the wildfire, the rose I gave
        my wife on our wedding day,
    the lilac bush in our backyard,

its blossoms opening on
    another spring, a door in
the earth of our marriage. Some-
        where someone sings the first few
    notes of "Mercy, Mercy Me"

& I can feel God cutting
    through submarine basilicas
of plankton & kelp, schools of
        krill swallowed in one large gulp,
    the whole baleen planet turned

pilot fish on a frigate's
    bow, the milky way become
a remora attached to
        a mako shark. I'm thinking
    about the infinity

in the period at the end
    of this sentence & the fact
I'm consuming natural
        resources each word I draft
    in ink on paper, each draft

I type on my laptop: trees
    ablaze, another forest
burning, another glacier
        melting, my daughter's, my son's—
    Bill, your grandchildren's—estate

measured out in snapdragons
    drowned & Queen Anne's lace bouquets
razed. Yes, our lives are lupine
        shoots in the Anthropocene,
    our epoch itself a lone

columbine among cowslips
    at the pasture's edge. Søren
Kierkegaard says a human
            being brings together time
    & eternity, freedom

& necessity. All good
    love songs bend orchids into
garlands, hold the finite
            in the unending. I trust
    in blue poppies, hummingbird

sage, my three-year-old's laughter,
    my wife in any blue hour,
& that each blade of sweetgrass,
            each lullaby, each thistle,
    each sorrow, each eel & worm

& river & raindrop, each grief,
    & every molecule in the fingertips
of the falsely accused, each
            dancing inch of our unjust
    world is worth pressing between

the pages of a *Collected Works*,
    a *New and Selected* made
of our bodies thrumming in
            the darkness—pterodactyl
    rose, fountaining overtures:

praise the biblical jaws, blue-
    tinged, frog spawn & fish, fathoms
deep, the amphibian curves
        of our predecessors' last
    wild thalassic sacred longings.

xvii. (interlude: Darwin's Arch)
Each night these days I dream of Earth
    ending. The planet implodes.
The iron & nickel in
        the core spurts out into space
    & auroras our former home.

This ending is beautiful
    in its way, a sudden flash
disintegrating canons
        & histories, the whole crush
    of human achievement gone

to comet, spinning off to
    uncharted interstellar
regions where an alien
        Shakespeare unsonnets & unquills
    the tentacled universe.

I've been reading my daughter
    too many volcano books.
The manta rays & hammerheads

          in my heart cut swiftly through
     rivers of bright red lava

in the atoms of stories
     I tell her before bedtime.
My wife is in those atoms,
          twenty-eight weeks pregnant with
     our second child & beaming,

wrapped up in Rapunzel's hair,
     along with the witches &
princesses & jellyfish
          & crabs wiggling through our minds
     as our child drifts off. She says,

"Don't talk, just tell the story:
     Once upon a time . . ." & once
again, I realize the world
          doesn't end. It just keeps on
     eroding into us, hour

by hour, one molecule at
     a time, paradise upon
paradise, Galápagos
          of endless want & need &
     give—yellowfin & turtle,

cormorant & albatross
     & eternal iguana

lounging in the good sunlight
        halfway around the globe from
    the elsewhere we dream ourselves

into, ashine like glints through
    whirling schools of angelfish.
These milliseconds, wingbeats, waves,
        flicker into us, lash us
    to the unknown, past the point

of undoing disaster:
    let us pray, as prairie dog
& clover & bee stitched into
        the vast eternal instant,
    for this Now I hold out to you.

xviii. (bright signatory)

While I paused in the writing
    of this poem, I read *Straight's*
Suite for Craig Cotter & Frank
        O'Hara, Bill, & realized
    how often your poetry

unfolds in direct address
    to other poets living
& dead, & so, how fitting
        an interlocutor I
    find you here with my unborn,

both in utero in some
 kind of way, suspended as
you & he are, on these steps,
 like Merwin's Hadrian's "little
 soul," a stray numinous burst.

Meanwhile, I've strayed. I meant to
 mention how in your *Straight's Suite*
you offer Richard Wilbur's
 assertion "that he's pretty
 sure his poem is done when

he's exhausted his present
 sense of subject." I wonder,
though I know what you both mean,
 if a present sense of
 subject might ever exhaust

itself inside a poem,
 & just now, Lucille Clifton
leapt to mind, her line "Sail through
 this to that," meaning heaven,
 paradise as departure

point & terminus, boat of
 such unknowing endless *Nows*,
tide that rolls out, in, cyclone
 boxed up & shipped off yonder
 like old country songs yodeled

by the wind into trembling
     thus & laddering a slake
of wants. Kierkegaard (again)
          said: "faith is a process of
     infinite becoming." I

say there's too much, not enough,
     infinity in this string
of words. I say faith is just
          an extra syllable in
     the throat of a line, a weird

enjambment of bleak ghosting
     a comfortable threadbare gray
old lack. I admit I am
          most rickety in my beliefs
     & think of God as a lung's

alveoli, those gates between
     air & bloodstream, & from such
thoughts, I intuit all time
          as stenciled words spray painted
     on brick, cutting the *y*'s off

eternity, cutting them off
     at the windpipe, at the hour
before image breaks to what?
          Bright signatory, cursive
     loping toward the endless

illegible, a desire,
    a name—mine, yours, his, hers, theirs?
a wind through lilac leaves,
        how poets graze & dream, gaze,
    & bow to the seraphim's fire.

xix. (the pomegranate's hundred hundred hearts)

At twenty-seven, you said:
    "My conflict, perhaps is simply
with the reality that
        all things eventually
    break up and die. What of two

raindrops in love?" You're thinking
    here about how to make home
where you are & not some lost
        & distant place, & you solved
    that problem in your poems

& in your life, I'm starting
    to see, by not allowing
the raindrops to divide, by
        letting the poem of home
    become a blackbird, winging

into poems on the page
    & in the air you exhaled,
in uranium atoms

split inside a redwing's beak,
in the great chain of being,

of wife & daughter & son
become one immutable
stanza, one quatrain against
despair & the vast blank &
unyielding nothing of death.

xx. (interlude: elegy for Eavan Boland)

Think of a poem as unassuming
as any suburb, anywhere
the world over, tenanted
with as many rabbits, cats,
widows, & mothers curling

up beside daughters & dads
& sons—& white minivans,
decaled with red stick figure
families on their rear windows—
with a leaf blower humming

a filleted garden music
voiceover to the trailer
for the movie your life might
be based on, the biopic
desire makes in the long hours

of Sunday afternoons, while
    a smell of honey ghosts your
nostrils, & you are confused
        about the very poem
    I just asked you to think up.

In middle age, you might look
    out an open skylight at
three a.m. & see Polaris
        shining & feel a hint of
    heaven, even as your life

reduces to a string of
    memories: of dry biscuits
& mutton, of bridal linens,
        a dense yew, a Renoir seen
    for a second & remembered

as a Degas, the impulse
    to defer acknowledgement
of a grief. A poem is
        a beautiful rift in time,
    begot in the throat's deep well.

Now think of Eavan Boland
    & your own (my own) rapidly
evanescing storyline.
        I am addressing the *You*
    that is *I* & *she* & *they*,

& the *us*, lonely & frail,
   in this holy difficult
Now. Hold the pomegranate's
       hundred hundred hearts in one
    hand, hold the glass king's courtiers

in the other. We were,
   like any poets, in love
with the gray undersides of
       mulberry leaves & the way
    the grass ekes toward twilight.

Our poems extrapolate
   paradise from the slip jig
of rain on paving stone. Hold
       close this long poem about
    a son of many fathers,

each father dying into
   his hundred hundred children,
rubied from hospital hallway
       to night-light to midnight moon
    & back again, to the gurney

with one wobbly wheel, veering
   toward the morgue on Thursday
in a Vallejo poem.
       These are the witnesses: wings
    pinned in a glass cubicle of sky.

xxi. (zero at the bone)

Bill, I was reading about
   the Sacoglossan sea slug,
which can cut off its own head
      & regenerate its body
   within three weeks. Scientists

call these decapitations
   autonomy, a function
most often used to escape
      predators; the starfish
   sheds an arm, sea cucumbers

eject internal organs,
   but this slug dismembers itself,
they think, to expel toxins,
      to untangle itself from
   the algae upon which it

feeds, & to rid itself from
   parasites. The head regrows
its body in twenty days
      & its old body wriggles
   on for awhile. Sometimes,

they shed more than one body
   in a lifetime, the way some
of us do (or wish we could).
      Yes, yes, I hear Emily:

If I feel physically

as if the top of my head
     were taken off, I know that . . .
I spend my days in poems
          & I have never felt that,
     but I would like to be as

intense as Emily with
     her loaded guns & narrow
fellows in the grass. I have
          syllables stuck in my throat
     & stars & crickets, but these

are not for poems alone.
     Those domains in her pockets
were scrawled on envelopes. Mine
          are typed into the soft light
     of a Dell, but come to think

of it, the moment my girl
     was born I felt the top of
my head come off & the first
          time I kissed my wife, & once
     in the moment my father

breathed his last breath as I carried
     him almost to the hospice
bed, I felt like I was cut,

disembodied, removed from
diastole, systole—

& this grief, this joy, was too
    much for one body to bear.
In a word: *autonomy*,
            a starfish, sea cucumbers,
    a Sacoglossan sea slug,

the heartbeat of a poem
    echoing, severed. That's why
I'm writing these words to you,
        my friend, with two outstretched hands
    in which I've placed my own head.

xxii. (in the manner of Proust & Tolstoy)
My memories parade
    themselves in outré brocades
of light, dividing my life
        in half: the *before her* &
    the *ever after else*s

groomed with luster, crabbed with fireworks
    dashed across a silk
of outsized tremulous sky.
        Love turns to anfractuous
    sentences unwinding from

the left margin. I'm always

translating myself into
myself. There's so much I'd like
        to call back & keep, saplings
    I'd like to unbend in time.

I am & was a deckle
    edge, a drawing room, an iris
blossoming distance under
        the eyelids of my unborn
    child, who is & is not me.

& blooming, thus: I gather
    my radiant manias
& sweet regrets & hold them
        out for you, these details that
    deepen into fond symbol.

The monk cloistered in my heart
    intoned me an embroidered
epic. Grief flew like blackbirds
        across an impossible
    winter tundra. Two cadets

dueled in my chest. A bleakness
    & its forgeries spun from
the fireplace to waltz embers
        away from me. What I mean is:
    I fell through the duchies of

turning page for a fortnight.

I knew, all too well, I could
live in this ancient city,
        a bear cub strapped to a cop
    & thrown into the river.

Your dragonfly eye darkens
    as you descend the spiral
staircase & enter genome,
            individual strand, all
    sides seen at once, these lines, steps

in the rain, under a toadstool,
    near moss & marsh & the twang
of banjo strings plucked by
            a pretty girl's calloused thumbs.
    I am woolgathering &

stargazing at fingerprints.
    I am a fox dreaming of
being a hedgehog, the whole
            fossil record telegraphed
    in the twitch of my whiskers.

xxiii. (interlude: prayer for Gaza)

I hone a heart on a heart
    inside me & it is sharp,
this heart, knife in the gut of
        a homeland, & this is not

a metaphor, neither this

image of heart on heart, nor
    the rockets launched, nor rubble,
nor blood in the streets. Look for
        a love poem to defend
    the sick moon against itself.

Look for a prayer that turns house-
    less doorways into salaams
of endless light. These are not
        figures of speech, these salaams
    & doorways. There is ruin

on the tongue when our talk turns
    to borders & nation states.
Gather the hummingbirds in
        your windpipe, let them ruby
    your throat a thousand thousand

wingbeats. Remember, to be
    human is to be broken
&, to be broken, is to
        see the almond blossom burst
    under the closed eyelids of

your beloved. Take them, by
    the waist, so gently. Let them
dance you to a place where our

         enjambments don't hemorrhage
     us into elsewhere & we

unearth ourselves into peace
     & the other azures of
infinite space unfolding
          in this whirling & this leap
     opening inside a palm.

xiv. (gleaming // a kind of rising)

Mid-morning, walking ocean
     shoreline, I found a hundred
blackbirds frozen in ice,
          only their heads protruding,
     black eyes open, gleaming, most

of their sharp beaks still,
     scissoring in mid-whistle.
To paraphrase Blake, blackbirds,
          which move some to tears of joy,
     are, in the eyes of others,

only a noisy shadow,
     which wavers in the way . . . As
a man is, so he sees. Bill,
          I think you are weeping
     as the blackbirds fly over
Brockport, back to Long Island,

into my basement & back
to the woods in a Hawthorne tale,
        flitting past Bartleby's desk
    as my unborn flips & kicks.

The aim of this poem is
    to speak to the *you* in *me*,
to the *me* in *you*, to say
        what matters most in its own
    music, as Galway Kinnell

said it best. In other words:
    these are words to other the ghosts.
A poem is a restorative
        utterance. A kind of "earned
    communion," Heaney said.

Stevens's resistance comes to
    mind too, & there are moments
when the rubber band snaps back,
        here against the wrist, so that
    the wrist becomes a river.

I river back to your blackbirds,
    Bill, & to you at the start
of your journal, Christmas day
        1964. John Coltrane
    recorded *A Love Supreme*
on the ninth of that month in

New Jersey, having composed
it in Dix Hills, not too far
            from your childhood home (and Walt's),
      those woods & farms & former

farmlands inspiring mystic
      reckonings with the sound of
the sound. You were twenty-four.
            Coltrane was thirty-seven.
      I was in the ether with

my son, daughter, wife, brother,
      & almost all my close friends.
When my son turns twenty-four,
            it'll be 2045.
      You'll be one hundred & five.

There are twenty-four sections
      in this poem, in honor of
the twenty-four blackbirds perched
            on its powerlines, cawing
      its images back into life.

My friend, Tom Bouman, once said,
      "a poet puts his business
in the street." My friend Nicole
            reminded me we're living
      in the era of amateur
Cat in the Hat tattoos. My friend

Leah wrote: "even in the
uneven, even in the
          today: julienne what you
     can—there are small raptures here."

My friend Faisal turned into
     a blackbird & his wingbeats
etched this phrase into the clouds:
          talk to other the ghosts. &
     I keep its braille in my heart.

You began your journal in
     another era. The entry
you began with gestured to
          the past & to the future,
     to this very line & to

Pepys whose diaries relate
     the daily arrhythmias
of life in the court & streets
          of seventeenth century
     England. You have no Newton

in your journals, but you have
     caught the arrhythmias
of the ordinary in
          the American grain as
     no one else has. When I was
twenty-four, I remember

reading an article on
Abu Ghraib while riding back
        to my apartment from class
    at the university,

a graduate seminar
    on the American novel
from 1945 to *Then*,
        which was *Present* in the course
    description. We read Faulkner,

Morrison, Bowles, Petry, Roth,
    Bulosan's *America Is*
in the Heart, Hagedorn's great
        Dogeaters about U.S.
    imperialism, Wright's

The Outsider, & a few
    more. *Tar Baby*'s spiraling
sentences were undoing
        me that day, that paragraph
    about the great masses of

undocumented men. Then,
    there was the pointed black hood
& the dog leash & I got
        off the bus and vomited
    on the sidewalk, while those still
on the bus probably thought

me a drunk underclassman
at five in the afternoon.
        & I knew then, there was this
    fugitive dark I couldn't

see, tightly interwoven
        in the stars and stripes. I felt
like I'd been punched in the gut,
            & it moved me to terror,
    more than 9/11 then,

because of the will to crush
        by deep humiliation,
because Jean Améry said
            torture is the essence of
    Nazism & your *Shoah*

Train & *Erika* bear that
        out. Kierkegaard reminds
us recollection causes
            unhappiness, but the same
    gesture in the opposite

direction makes one happy—
        repetition rather than,
repetition rather than,
            recollection is what all
    poems, this one included,

should aspire to—& that's why

there are so many Kierkegaards
& fetuses & blackbirds
  & larynxes & open
throats & apples & stairwells

in this poem. How many
 Hiroshimas must we
endure? How many Trident
   missiles must detonate in
our cerebellums? How many

9/11s? How many drone
 strikes? How many innocent
bystanders gunned down by lone
   wolf assassins in our streets?
 How much nostalgic bile

can we choke back? There's no apt
 rejoinder to those questions,
except to embrace the way
   our poems reprise the best
echoes of us & our days.

I hate to talk *us* & *we*
 in any poem, but there is
this drive to put in motion
   E. M. Forster's epigraph
 to *Howards End*, a novel

about urban sprawl, prefaced with:

Only connect. Those words sear me.
I see my father's face in
      them, & so, I see my own
   & my son's, our expression

a stone skipping the surface
   of the Susquehanna at
dawn, those mornings I would walk
      down to its confluence with
   the Chenango & look for

poetry after staying
   up all night pursuing it
through dog-eared copies of Frost,
      Stevens, Ashbery, Ginsberg,
   Ferlinghetti, Hikmet, Hall,

Clifton, Coleman, Knight, Donne, Smart,
   Tennyson, Dickinson, Walt,
Schuyler, Pound, all the Williams
      except for you (I came to
   you later), Baraka, Pound,

Vallejo, Lorca, Dickey,
   Neruda, Wilbur, Stafford,
Plath, Wright, Sexton, Ammons, Koch,
      Lehman, Espada, Rumi,
   Bei Dao, Issa, Rukeyser,

Wheatley, Broadstreet, Edson, Wright,

Larkin, Moore, Kunitz, Bishop,
Roethke, Kinnell, Yeats, Heaney,
        Lowell, Hayes, Gilbert, Simic,
    Hayden, Lawrence, O'Hara,

Akhmatova, Kessler, Bronk,
    Berryman, Szymborska,
Borges, Miłosz, Kavanaugh,
        Marie Howe, Hopkins, Hopkins,
    Hopkins, more Hopkins. This list,

my litany of the saints,
    this incomplete list of lives
cascading through my poems
        & into my life, my lives,
    their rhythms repeated in

mine, their sounds & sense tingling
    in my fingertips & ears.
I think of your music, Bill,
        & Harvey Hix's project
    to test the assertion that:

"Poetry in this time &
    nation is doing the work of
philosophy" (according
        to Leslie Scalapino).
    I am back to first questions.

I don't want a poem to

work at doing. Instead, it
should embody its own kind
        of undoing, the kind of
    loosening that occurs when

you walk into the house at
    the end of a long day of
work & your family is
        there, or they're soon to be home,
    a reunification, now

& then repeated daily.
    You once wrote that a new poem
surely *will unlearn itself*
        to extinction, but then start
    again anew, a starfish

reconstellating itself
    among the kelp & dreaming
the light of a dying star
        in its tiny ossicles
    as the sea roars far above.

Soon, we will begin again
    anew together (by *we*
I mean I & I mean
        my son & wife & daughter)
    just as you did & still do,

Bill. I hope that if I live

to be eighty, I'll be like
you, writing more & better
          poems, the late work as good,
     if not greater, than what came

before. Three days before I
     was born, you wrote of the concerns
you had in penning a long
          poem: "balances of dream/
     waking" to be carried forth

& reconciled. I feel that way
     now, on the stairs, picturing
you writing in your easy
          chair, while your wife is asleep
     (she's sick, you wrote, & I hope

she's feeling better as I
     write these words). & it occurs
to me, again, how timebound
          this particular poem
     is, & how okay I am

with that. One of the things that
     always irked me about
your contemporaries was
          how dead set they all were on
     eternity, but I guess

poets of my age could use

an unadulterated
hit of ambition. I think
        of that essay by Donald
        Hall, where he gives the writing

assignment: "Be as good a
        poet as George Herbert. Take
as long as you wish." He said,
        "The grander goal is to be
        as good as Dante." That joke

is between my son & I. Here's
        another one: a middle-
aged man, a spry retiree,
        & a fetus walk into
        a bar & order three vespers

(or were they three old-fashioneds?) . . .
        I don't much like alcohol
in poems or in poets,
        though I understand, when you
        were young, those were different

times, still I don't think I could
        tolerate Berryman or
Dickey, no matter how much
        I admire their poetry.
        Honestly, though I would have

put up with them, probably.

I'm sometimes disappointed
when a poet I meet is
    a jerk, but then I have to
    remind myself that poets

are not their poems. It's like
    the soul in the mysticism
of Saint Hildegard. She says
       the body is in the soul,
    not the other way around,

the way most people think. So,
    too, the poet is always
in the poem. The poem
       is never in the poet.
    That's why we can meet right here

on the stairs, holding our loves
    in our hands like bouquets or
the shards of shipwrecked vases in
       a John Frederick Nims poem
    my wife loves, holding each to

each, & building outward, full
    of stars & redolent
with the smell of freshly cut
       grass in the suburbs where ghosts
    become rabbits, become kings

& queens waiting for the rain

to paint their selves into scenes
imagined in the mind of
 a rabid fox waiting for
the farmer's bullet beside

the tombstone of a graveyard
 on a family farm, miles
to the south of wherever
 whomever reads this, finds
 themselves awake and dreaming.

I dream again your blackbirds:
 Feeding, they'd been caught in sea-
spray, must be—all males, up
 north early, scarlet epaulettes
 aflame a few inches under.

I chipped one bird loose with gloved
 hands, under the rising sun
until, until I realized,
 until I realized nothing
 I hadn't known. The tide

retreated & would return.
 Within the austere territories
these would have filled with belligerence
 & song, spring had begun. Bill,
 your great poem here rewritten,

verbatim, but not transcribed

exactly, instead, transformed,
re-lineated as steps
            in this staircase, but turning
      like that prophetic gyre in

Yeats, turning as images
      only can, into a flock,
into pure flight, into sound
            & sense, the stippled contours
      of a life. Your life in one

great image, great as any
      image in Dante, Dante,
& Dante—greater even,
            these blackbirds I cup here
      in my naked palms, as I go

with you, to shoreline & sound,
      carrying our litanies,
tribes, vernaculars, passwords,
            back to a frozen instant,
      back to the origin of song,

back through this spiral stairwell.
      This is the twenty-fourth part
of the poem, the end of our
            day together. The night
      comes on like a blackbird. Bill,

I like your blackbirds more than

Stevens's misprisioned thirteen
drawn into one crow stuck in
       Crazy Jane's craw as she talks
   to Elizabeth Bishop.

Listen, Ishmael Reed chants
   and augurs seven blackbirds
against the slur in Stevens's
       "C," which is the slur inside
  a supreme fiction undone

by a blackbird's orison.
   We, with our pandemics, sleeves
rolled up & vaccinated,
       one nation fused to protest,
  efflorescing poetry

in a thousand twitter feeds,
   in a thousand blackbird beaks,
we delicate dreaming ones,
       little boxes of dust in
  a dead Ohioan's words . . .

Bill, what is this writing life
   good for? I expect your
answer is the life put down
       in volume after volume,
  how, like Kunitz said, life is

always dying into poems,

as poems always die into
our lives, but dying might be
   understood as a kind of
  rising, in the way he said it,

or, at least, a kind of rapture
  bleeding out, a blotting dab
at the watercolor edge.
   As in: Look at the blackbirds bled
  out along the horizon,

blackbirds flying in patterns
  that recall a pointillist
self-portrait I did at twelve.
   The blackbirds sing my sinews
  into motion. The platelets

in my veins echo their caws.
  I can hear them in your lines.
& now I've gone far afield.
   My wife was born in Smithtown
  where you attended high school,

but, so what, again? I think
  I've lost control of this train
of thought, written in pencil,
   the *m* after *m* a flock
  of blackbirds alighting on

loose-leaf, apparition of

my boyhood self, scribbling out
long comic strips featuring
    a bumbling superhero
  version of myself, trying

to save the whole planet. Here
  I am again, nobody,
a poem myself, & you,
     doubling our twice-scissored selves,
    scissoring in mid-whistle—

envoi (a traveler's prayer)

In a poem, a son moves
  into his father & turns
him into a new country
     with a reconceived heartland.
  There is no talk of birthrate,

no debate about childcare
  & immigration. Borders,
in a poem, are porous.
     & sons & fathers & wives
    & daughters migrate like swifts

& butterflies or like bees
  pollinating a prairie.
They pattern their flights on earth
    & wind & water & dark

from the most distant starlight

born two galaxies away.
My friend Faisal writes his son
inside a house, a castle,
        the world, another poem
        exhaled from Allah's right lung.

Meanwhile, my unborn son floats
        in amniotic fluid,
a cosmonaut ascending
        the sable warmth of the womb.
        My own father has been dead,

sparrowing in his grave now
        for years. I can feel myself
moving in him even as
        I can feel my son kicking
        in my wife's belly at night.

These motions don't dissipate
        with death & its ripe fictions.
A baby's DNA stays
        in its mother forever,
        my wife tells me. I think of

those helixes inscribing
        their ardent calligraphies
in elegant unruly ink

on my wife's hemoglobin
as we raise our two children.

Just so, we poets remain
in our lines, our atoms etched
in each enjambment, riding
the rhythms that unwind there,
rewriting each beat as it

orbits away from the hand
that wrote it, from the open
throat about to burst into
song. O poets (sons, daughters):
we are truly holy when

it is difficult for us
to tell, among the many places
we have lived, precisely where
it was we felt most at home.
This is the knowledge God gives:

family is rootless prayer—
those helixes inscribing
their ardent calligraphies
in elegant unruly ink—
family is rootless prayer.

Acknowledgments

Thank you to the editors and staff of the following publications in which sections of this poem have appeared, sometimes in different versions: *Beloit Poetry Journal, Brilliant Corners, Paterson Literary Review, Presence,* and *Rock & Sling.*

Section xvi. (after Anthony Brunelli's *Depot at Dusk*) appeared in the Arnot Art Museum as part of the exhibit *High Fidelity: Anthony Brunelli and the Digital Age Photorealists.*

Thank you to Ron Wallace and Sean Bishop for championing this book. Thank you to Dennis Lloyd, Jacqueline Nora Krass, Alison Shay, Jennifer Conn, Jessica Smith, and the staff at the University of Wisconsin Press for bringing it into the world. Thank you to Phil Brady, Bob Mooney, Maria Mazziotti Gillan, and Harvey Hix for their continued support of my poetry. Thank you to Alison C. Rollins, Richard Blanco, and Chloé Firetto-Toomey. Thank you to Liz Rosenberg for assigning Galway Kinnell's *The Book of Nightmares* in her undergraduate poetry workshop so many years ago. Thank you to William Heyen for lighting my way. Thank you to my friends, family, teachers, and students (past, present, and future). Thank you to my daughter, Luciana, and to my son, Dante, the greatest poems I will ever know by heart. Thank you, most of all, to my wife, Christina, the best whistler I know, and the one who braids together all my competing melodies.

᯾

Notes

William Heyen is the author of more than forty books of poetry and prose. His life and work incited this poem, especially *The Cabin: Journal 1964–1984* (H_NGM_N Books, 2012), *To William Merwin: A Poem* (Mammoth Books, 2007), and *Nature: Selected and New Poems 1970–2020* (Mammoth Books, 2021). Heyen's advice inspired the form the poem took. All quotes from Heyen's body of work in this volume appear with his permission.

ii. (an *Unyet* just begun): The quote from Franz Kafka is taken from *The Diaries of Franz Kafka: 1910–1923* (Schocken Books, 1988).

iv. (this mattering of music): The phrase "talk to other the ghosts" comes from an unpublished poem by Faisal Mohyuddin titled "All Day Today I Felt Like a Heartsick Traveler."

v. (soundtrack for a zombie apocalypse): This section references and draws inspiration from Eddie Hazel, guitarist for Funkadelic; William Faulkner and his home in Oxford, Mississippi; Robert Kirkman's *The Walking Dead*; and Spike Lee's *BlacKkKlansman*.

viii. (poetry, be my body of shining): The poem mentioned at the end of this section originally appeared in William Heyen's *Crazy Horse & the Custers* (Nine Point Publishing, 2015). Heyen sent me the poem, handwritten on the back of a baseball-card-sized reproduction of a DeLoss McGraw painting. The poem was encased in one of the hard plastic sleeves used by collectors to protect baseball cards during the 1990s.

ix. (a forty-three-second free fall): The quotes in this section come from *The Cabin: Journal 1964–1984* (H_NGM_N Books, 2012) and from an interview of Heyen conducted by Philip Brady for *Artful Dodge*.

xvi. (after Anthony Brunelli's *Depot at Dusk*): Anthony Brunelli (b. 1968) is a photorealist painter from Binghamton, New York. This section of the poem unfolds in dialogue with Brunelli's painting *Depot at Dusk*, 2016–17, oil on polyester, 40 × 72 in., 101.6 × 182.9 cm.

xxiii. (interlude: prayer for Gaza): The italicized lines that begin this section come from Yehuda Amichai's poem "The Travels of Benjamin the Last, of Tudela."

xiv. (gleaming // a kind of rising): The friends mentioned by first name alone in this section are the poets Nicole Santalucia, Leah Umansky, and Faisal Mohyuddin. Tom Bouman is a crime fiction writer, author of the Henry Farrell novels. The quote from Leah Umansky comes from her collection *The Barbarous Century* (Eyewear Publishing, 2018).

envoi (a traveler's prayer): This section responds to Faisal Mohyuddin's poem "Allah Castles" and owes a debt to the following passage from Paul Bowles's novel *The Sheltering Sky*: "Whereas the tourist generally hurries back home at the end of a few weeks or months, the traveler, belonging no more to one place than to the next, moves slowly, over periods of years, from one part of the earth to another. Indeed, he would have found it difficult to tell, among the many places he had lived, precisely where it was he had felt most at home."

Wisconsin Poetry Series

Sean Bishop and Jesse Lee Kercheval, series editors
Ronald Wallace, founding series editor

(B) = Winner of the Brittingham Prize in Poetry
(FP) = Winner of the Felix Pollak Prize in Poetry
(4L) = Winner of the Four Lakes Prize in Poetry

Dante Di Stefano is the author of the poetry collections *Love Is a Stone Endlessly in Flight* (2016); *Ill Angels* (2019); and *Lullaby with Incendiary Device*, published in a three-in-one collection titled *Generations* (2022), which also features work by William Heyen and H. L. Hix. His poetry, essays, and reviews have appeared in *Best American Poetry 2018*, *Prairie Schooner*, the *Sewanee Review*, the *Writer's Chronicle*, and elsewhere. He has won the On Teaching Poem Prize, the Manchester Poetry Prize (UK), the Red Hen Press Poetry Award, the Thayer Fellowship in the Arts, the Ruth Stone Poetry Prize, and the Allen Ginsberg Poetry Award, as well as prizes from the Academy of American Poets, *Crab Orchard Review*, the *Madison Review*, the *Southern Humanities Review*, and *Stone Canoe*. Along with María Isabel Álvarez, he coedited the anthology *Misrepresented People: Poetic Responses to Trump's America* (2018). He holds a PhD in English literature from Binghamton University. He teaches high school English in Endicott, New York, and lives in Endwell, New York, with his wife, Christina, their daughter, Luciana, their son, Dante Jr., and their goldendoodle, Sunny.